Easy Crock Pot Cookbook

Yummy every day recipes for beginners and advanced. Enjoy wholesome low fat dishes. Lower Blood pressure, regain confidence and reset metabolism with 50 amazing recipes

Clara Smith

Table of Contents

Introduction

The crockpot slow cooking method involves basically depositing the ingredients you desire to cook into the crockpot bowl (usually by stirring it with a wooden spoon or a ladle), adding the liquid of choice, cooking it for a few hours until it's done. These used to be the standard cooking methods in kitchens, and they have stayed the same with the invention of the crockpot. Nowadays, most crockpots have interiors thermostatically controlled to ensure that it's set at the right temperature during the cooking process to not over-cook your meals.

The best in crockpot slow cooking is finding that low and slow recipe. Recipes that are low in time length are usually very low in steps, and not much work is involved. It usually leads to the much sought after 'set it and forget it' kind of meal. Imagine not having to watch your meals cook slowly as you work on other tasks; you can avoid the temptation of peeking or checking on it too often and not having to worry about burning or crusting on the sides of your crockpot. When cooking at low heat, you don't have to worry about your meal exploding all over the kitchen or all the grease falling out and sticking to the bottom of your crock.

The best use of crockpot slow cooking is the convenience of the food, especially during holidays and parties. You can set the crockpot down on the table, and everyone can serve themselves. It is an excellent and great way to spend time with your guests and treat them well. There is nothing cheesier than eating the same dish fondue style. You get to enjoy slow cooking hotdogs for hours and hours without little ones surreptitiously taking off the top and poaching them in the pool of oil sitting beside the dish.

A crockpot is a very good way to use leftovers for a delicious meal. If you cook a large meal regularly and you have leftovers, put them in a crockpot with a liquid and let it cook. It will double the amount of food leftover or fed to the cat at the end of the week.

Crockpot cooking generally saves time, but it is also a low-budget way to cook. Slow cooking food can save you money because they are usually very low and easy to make. In fact, it is even possible to cook a meal with the last few pennies in your wallet. If you're on a tight budget and you don't have much to spend on your meals, the crockpot is the way to go.

Crockpots even make for a great gift since it's made in many shapes and sizes, from the really small, 1-quart crockpot to the huge 8 quarts or more. Any shape or size would be a welcome gift for anyone because everyone eats. Any occasion could be a good time to give someone a crockpot, and the more occasions you can name, the more crockpots you could make as gifts.

Crockpots are a good thing for singles who do not have many friends, and getting together can be difficult. You can go on cooking and not having to worry about cooking for anyone. You also don't have to go through the motions of doing a dinner party or charity work every week. You could just throw some ingredients together in your crockpot, turn it on and leave. That way, you're free to do whatever you like while your crockpot cooks your meal.

To whom is this cookbook? This cookbook is for people who want to spend less time in the kitchen and less money on food. This cookbook is also for people who wish to cook their meals in a healthy manner or for people with little time or money, and lastly, this is for people who enjoy sharing meals with friends and family. Treat your guests to a good meal every day. Slow cooking, live long!

CHAPTER 1:

Breakfast

1.   Cauliflower Casserole

Preparation Time: 10 minutes Cooking Time: 6 hours

Servings: 8

Ingredients:

- 12 eggs

- 1/2 cup unsweetened almond milk

- 1 lb. sausage, cooked and crumbled

- 1 cauliflower head, shredded

- 2 cups cheddar cheese, shredded

- Pepper

- Salt

Directions:

1. Spray a crock pot inside with cooking spray. In a bowl, whisk together eggs, almond milk, pepper, and salt.

2. Add about a third of the shredded cauliflower into the bottom of the crock pot. Season with pepper and salt. Top with about a third of the sausage and a third of the cheese.

3. Repeat the same layers 2 more times. Pour egg mixture into the crock pot. Cover and cook on low for 6 hours. Serve and enjoy.

Nutrition:Calories 443 Fat 35.6 g Carbohydrates 3.5 g Protein 27.4 g

2.   Lemon Cinnamon Apples

Preparation Time: 10 minutes

Cooking Time: 3 hours

Servings: 10

Ingredients:

- 9 cups apple, peeled, cored, diced

- 2 tbsp fresh lemon juice

- 1/2 tsp nutmeg

- 2 tsp ground cinnamon 1 1/2 cups water

Directions:

1. Add all ingredients to a crock pot and stir well. Cover
   and cook on high for 3 hours. Stir well and serve.

Nutrition:Calories 50 Fat 0.2 g arbohydrates 13.1 g Protein
0.3 g

3. Egg, Kale, And Mozzarella Casserole

Preparation Time: 5 minutes

Cooking Time: 4 hours

Servings: 6

Ingredients:

- 5 ounces kale leaves, rinsed then chopped

- 2 teaspoons olive oil

- 1 ½ cup mozzarella cheese, grated

- 1/3 cup green onions, sliced

- 8 eggs, beaten

Directions:

1. Mix all ingredients in a bowl and stir to combine all ingredients. Place in a Ziploc bag and write the date when the recipe is made. Place inside the freezer.

2. Once you are ready to cook the meal, allow to thaw on the countertop for at least 2 hours. Place in the crockpot. Close the lid and cook on low for 4 hours or on high for 2 hours.

Nutrition:

Calories: 284

Carbohydrates: 3.2g

Protein: 28.1g

Fat: 31.4g

4. Pesto Scrambled Eggs

Preparation time: 5 minutes

Cooking time: 4 hours

Servings: 3

Ingredients:

- 3 large eggs, beaten

- 1 tablespoon butter

- 1 tablespoon organic green pesto sauce

- 2 tablespoon sour cream, full-fat

- Salt and pepper to taste

Directions:

1. In a mixing bowl, combine all ingredients. Place in a Ziploc bag and write the date when the recipe is made. Place inside the freezer.

2. Once you are ready to cook the meal, allow to thaw on the countertop for at least 2 hours. Place in the crockpot.

3. Close the lid and cook on high for 2 hours or on low for 4 hours. Halfway before the cooking time, use fork to break the eggs into small pieces. Continue cooking until eggs are well done.

Nutrition:

Calories: 467

Carbohydrates: 3.3g

Protein: 20.4g

Fat: 41.5g

5. Kale and Cheese Omelet

Preparation time: 15 minutes

Cooking time: 4 hours

Servings: 2

Ingredients:

- 5 eggs, beaten

- 2 tablespoons onion, chopped

- 2 teaspoons olive oil

- 3 ounces kale, chopped

- 1/3 cup white cheese, grated

Directions:

1. Mix all ingredients in a bowl. Place in a Ziploc bag and write the date when the recipe is made. Place inside the freezer.

2. Once you are ready to cook the meal, allow to thaw on the countertop for at least 2 hours. Place all ingredients in the crockpot. Cook on high for 2 hours or on low for 3 hours.

Nutrition:

Calories: 372

Carbohydrates: 2.1g

Protein: 24.5g

Fat: 36.2g

CHAPTER 2:

Mains

6.   Zesty Chicken Barbeque

Preparation time: 11 minutes

Cooking time: 8 hours

Servings: 6

Ingredients:

- Chicken breast halves

- Italian salad dressing

- 2 tbsp. Worcestershire sauce

- 1 bottle barbeque sauce

- Brown sugar

Directions:

1. Grease your crock pot with special cooking spray. Remove the bones and skin of chicken. Place the chicken into your crock pot.

2. In a bowl, combine Italian salad dressing, barbeque sauce, Worcestershire sauce, brown sugar. Pour the sauce mix over the chicken. Cover and prepare on high for 3-4 hour, or on low for 8 hours.

Nutrition:

Calories: 300

Fat: 8g

Carbohydrates: 32g

Protein: 23g

7.　Chicken with Dumplings

Preparation time: 13 minutes

Cooking time: 6 hours

Servings: 9

Ingredients:

- chicken breast halves

- 1 onion

- 2 cans condensed cream of chicken soup

- Butter

- 2 packs biscuit dough

Directions:

1. Remove the skin from chicken. Finely dice the onion. Grease your crock pot with some butter. Place the

chicken into crock pot. Cover with diced onion, cream of chicken soup, butter. Pour in some water.

2. Prepare during 5 hours on high mode. When it is 30 minutes before serving, place the torn biscuit into the dish.

Nutrition:

Calories: 387

Fat: 10g

Carbohydrates: 38g

Protein: 12g

8.   Beef Roast

Preparation time: 19 minutes

Cooking time: 6 hours

Servings: 9

Ingredients:

- Bone-in beef roast

- Medium onion

- Sliced mushrooms

- Vegetable oil

- Salt/pepper

- Chicken broth

- 1 tbsp. tomato paste

- 2 sprigs thyme

- 3 medium carrots

- 2 cloves garlic

- Simple flour

- Celery

- 1 sprig rosemary (fresh)

- 1 tbsp. butter

Directions:

1. Season the roast from all sides with salt and pepper. Sprinkle a little with flour just to cover. Heat the vegetable oil in a large frying pan and brown the meat evenly.

2. Add butter and mushrooms, cook for 5 minutes. Then, stir in garlic, onion, 1-tablespoon flour and tomato paste. Slowly stir in chicken stock and let to simmer.

3. Cut the carrots and celery. Then place to crock pot along with roast and other vegetables, thyme and rosemary. Pour the mushroom mixture. Cook on low for 5-6 hours.

Nutrition:

Calories: 777

Fat: 57g

Carbohydrates: 7g

Protein: 754g

9. Seasoned Beef with Cream

Preparation time: 16 minutes

Cooking time: 5 hours

Servings: 8

Ingredients:

- Lean ground beef

- 5 tbsp. milk

- 1/2 cup waters

- 1 pack dry au jus mix

- 2 tbsp. vegetable oil

- 3 tbsp. flour

- 1/2 cup Italian seasoned bread crumbs

- Dry onion soup mix

- 2 cans condensed cream of chicken soup

Directions:

1. In a separate and large bowl combine the beef, bread crumbs, onion soup mix, milk. Stir with hands. Separate the mixture into 8 parts and form the patties out of them.

2. Heat the vegetable oil in a large frying pan and quickly cook the patties until brown. Transfer the patties into greased crock pot dish.

3. In a separate bowl, combine au jus mix, cream of chicken soup, water. Pour into crock pot. Cook on low temperature for 4-5 hours.

Nutrition: Calories: 388 Fat: 24g Carbohydrates: 18g Protein: 23g

CHAPTER 3:

Sides

10.   Glazed Spiced Carrots

Preparation Time: 10 minutes

Cooking Time: 8 hours

Servings: 6

Ingredients:

- 2 lbs. small carrots

- 1/2 cup of peach preserves

- 1/2 cup of butter, melted

- 1/4 cup of packed brown swerve

- 1 teaspoon of vanilla extract

- 1/2 teaspoon of cinnamon, ground

- 1/4 teaspoon of salt

- 1/8 teaspoon of ground nutmeg

- 2 tablespoons of xanthan gum

- 2 tablespoons of water

- Toasted diced pecans, optional

Directions:

1. Start by throwing all the fixings into the Crockpot. Cover its lid and cook for 8 hours on Low setting.

2. Once done, remove its lid of the crockpot carefully. Mix well and garnish as desired. Serve warm.

Nutrition: Calories 220 Fat 20.1 g Carbs 63 g Protein 6.1 g

11.   Garlic Green Beans with Gorgonzola

Preparation Time: 10 minutes

Cooking Time: 4 hours

Servings: 6

Ingredients:

- 2 lbs. fresh green beans, halved

- 1 can (8 oz.) sliced chestnuts, drained

- 4 green onions, diced

- 5 bacon strips, cooked and crumbled, divided

- 1/3 cup of white wine

- 2 tablespoons of minced fresh thyme

- 4 garlic cloves, minced

- 1 1/2 teaspoons of seasoned salt

- 1 cup of (8 oz.) sour cream

- 3/4 cup of crumbled Gorgonzola cheese

Directions:

1. Start by throwing all the fixings into the Crockpot except cheese and bacon. Cover its lid and cook for 4 hours on Low setting.

2. Once done, remove its lid of the crockpot carefully. Mix well and garnish with bacon and cheese. Serve warm.

Nutrition:

Calories 331

Fat 32.9 g

Carbs 9.1 g

Protein 4.4 g

12. Green Beans

Preparation Time: 10 minutes

Cooking Time: 3 hours

Servings: 16

Ingredients:

- 16 cups of frozen French-style green beans, thawed

- 1/2 cup of butter, melted

- 1/2 cup of packed brown swerve

- 1 1/2 teaspoons of garlic salt

- 3/4 teaspoon of soy sauce

Directions:

1. Start by throwing all the fixings into the Crockpot. Cover its lid and cook for 3 hours on Low setting.

2. Once done, remove its lid of the crockpot carefully. Mix well and garnish as desired. Serve warm.

Nutrition:

Calories 237

Fat 22 g

Carbs 5 g

Protein 5 g

13. Party Sausages

Preparation Time: 10 minutes

Cooking Time: 2 hours

Servings: 16

Ingredients:

- 2 lbs. smoked sausage links, sliced diagonally

- 1 bottle (8 oz.) Catalina salad dressing

- 1 bottle (8 oz.) Russian salad dressing

- 1/2 cup of packed brown swerve

- 1/2 cup of apple cider

- Sliced green onions, optional

Directions:

1. Start by throwing all the fixings into the Crockpot. Cover its lid and cook for 2 hours on Low setting.

2. Once done, remove its lid of the crockpot carefully. Mix well and garnish as desired. Serve warm.

Nutrition:

Calories 190

Fat 17.25 g

Carbs 5.5 g

Protein 23 g

14.   Collard Greens

Preparation Time: 10 minutes

Cooking Time: 10 hours

Servings: 6

Ingredients:

- 4 bunches collard greens, trimmed and diced

- 1 lb. ham shanks

- 4 pickled jalapeno peppers, diced

- 1/2 teaspoon of baking soda

- 1 teaspoon of olive oil

- black pepper to taste

- garlic powder to taste

- ¼ cup of vegetable stock

Directions:

1. Start by throwing all the fixings into the Crockpot. Cover its lid and cook for 10 hours on Low setting.

2. Once done, remove its lid of the crockpot carefully. Mix well and garnish as desired. Serve warm.

Nutrition:

Calories 121

Fat 12.9 g

Carbs 8.1 g

Protein 5.4 g

CHAPTER 4:

Seafood

15.   Poached Salmon Salad

Preparation time: 15 minutes

Cooking time: 1 hour & 30 minutes

Servings: 4 Ingredients:

- 1 pound salmon fillets

- 1 teaspoon salt

- 1 teaspoon black pepper

- 1 cup chicken stock

- ¼ cup dry white wine

- ¼ cup capers

- 1 tablespoon fresh dill, chopped

- 4 cups fresh spinach

- ¼ cup crème fraiche

Directions:

1. Season the salmon with salt and black pepper, and then place the salmon in the crock pot. Combine the chicken stock and white wine and pour it over the salmon.

2. Add the capers and fresh dill. Cover and cook on low for 1 ½ hours, or until cooked through. Arrange fresh spinach on serving plates and top with cooked salmon. Garnish with a dollop of crème fraiche when serving.

Nutrition:Calories 231 Fat 9.4 g Carbs 2.1 g Protein 30.6 g

16.   Shrimp Diablo

Preparation time: 15 minutes

Cooking time: 6 hours

Servings: 4

Ingredients:

- 1 spaghetti squash (approximately 2 cups when cooked)

- 1 cup onion, sliced

- 4 cloves garlic, crushed and minced

- 1 cup chicken or seafood stock

- 1 teaspoon salt

- 1 teaspoon black pepper

- 1 pound shrimp, cleaned and deveined

- ¼ cup butter, melted

- 1 tablespoon crushed red pepper flakes

- 1 teaspoon cayenne powder

- 1 teaspoon oregano

- 1 tablespoon lemon juice

Directions:

1. Using a fork or sharp knife, poke 12-15 holes or small cuts in the surface of the spaghetti squash and place it in the center of the crock pot.

2. Add the onion, garlic, chicken stock, salt, and black pepper around the squash. Cover, and cook on low for 6 hours. Remove the spaghetti squash from the crock pot and turn the heat to high.

3. Allow the squash to cool just enough to handle before cutting it in half and scooping the insides back into the crock pot. Discard the empty shell.

4. Give the contents of the crock pot a quick toss to mix the ingredients. Add the shrimp, melted butter, crushed red pepper flakes, cayenne powder, oregano, and lemon juice to the crock pot.

5. Cover and cook 10-15 minutes, or until the shrimp are cooked through.

Nutrition:

Calories 252.7

Fat 13.1 g

Carbs 8.7 g

Protein 25 g

17.   Curried Shrimp and Cabbage

Preparation time: 15 minutes

Cooking time: 4 hours & 15 minutes

Servings: 4 Ingredients:

- 4 cups cabbage, shredded

- 1 cup onion, sliced thin

- 2 cloves garlic, crushed and minced

- 1 tablespoon curry powder

- 1 teaspoon salt

- 1 teaspoon black pepper

- 1 cup chicken or fish stock

- 1 cup coconut milk

- 1 pound shrimp, cleaned and deveined

- ¼ cup butter, melted

- ¼ cup full fat yogurt

- ¼ cup fresh cilantro, chopped

Directions:

1. Place the cabbage, onion, garlic, curry powder, salt, and black pepper in a crock pot and toss to mix. Next, add the chicken or fish stock and coconut milk.

2. Cover and cook on high for 4 hours. Remove the lid from the crock pot and add the shrimp, melted butter, and yogurt.

3. Cover and cook an additional 10-15 minutes, or until the shrimp is cooked through. Garnish with fresh cilantro before serving.

Nutrition:

Calories 274.7 Fat 14.8 g Carbs 9.7 g Protein 26.3 g

18.   Creamy Bay Scallops

Preparation time: 15 minutes

Cooking time: 2 hours & 55 minutes

Servings: 4 Ingredients:

- ¼ cup butter

- 1 tablespoon shallots, diced

- ¼ cup dry white wine

- 1 tablespoon lemon juice

- 2 cups mushrooms, quartered

- ¼ cup fresh parsley, chopped

- ½ cup heavy cream

- ¼ cup crème fraiche

- 1 teaspoon salt

- 1 teaspoon black pepper

- 1 pound bay scallops

- ½ cup Gruyere cheese, cubed

Directions:

1. Combine the butter, shallots, white wine, and lemon juice in a crock pot. Cover and cook on high for 2 hours.

2. Remove the lid from the crock pot and add the mushrooms, parsley, heavy cream, crème fraiche, salt, and black pepper.

3. Mix well, cover, and cook for 5-10 minutes to bring the heat of the liquid back up. Add the scallops and Gruyere cheese. Cook an additional 30-35 minutes, or until the scallops are cooked through.

Nutrition: Calories 420.8 Fat 32 g Carbs 5.6 g Protein 25.3 g

19. Chipotle Salmon Fillets

Preparation Time: 15 minutes

Cooking time: 2 hours

Servings: 2

Ingredients:

- 2 medium salmon fillets, boneless

- A pinch of nutmeg, ground

- A pinch of cloves, ground

- A pinch of ginger powder

- Salt and black pepper to the taste

- 2 tsp sugar

- 1 tsp onion powder

- ¼ tsp chipotle chili powder

- ½ tsp cayenne pepper

- ½ tsp cinnamon, ground

- 1/8 tsp thyme, dried

Directions:

1. Place the salmon fillets in foil wraps. Drizzle ginger, cloves, salt, thyme, cinnamon, black pepper, cayenne, chili powder, onion powder, nutmeg, and coconut sugar on top.

2. Wrap the fish fillet with aluminum foil. Put the crockpot's lid on and set the cooking time to 2 hours over low heat. Unwrap the fish and serve warm.

Nutrition: Calories 220 Fat 4g Carbs 7g Protein 4g

20.   Cod and Broccoli

Preparation Time: 15 minutes

Cooking time: 3 hours

Servings: 2

Ingredients:

- 1 pound cod fillets, boneless

- 1 cup broccoli florets

- ½ cup veggie stock

- 2 tablespoons tomato paste

- 2 garlic cloves, minced

- 1 red onion, minced

- ½ teaspoon rosemary, dried

- A pinch of salt and black pepper

- 1 tablespoon chives, chopped

Directions:

1. In your crockpot, mix the cod with the broccoli, stock, tomato paste, and the other ingredients, toss, put the lid on and cook on Low for 3 hours. Divide the mix between plates and serve.

Nutrition:

Calories 200

Fat 13g

Carbs 6g

Protein 11g

CHAPTER 5:

Poultry

21. Buttered Rosemary Chicken Breasts

Preparation time: 8 minutes

Cooking time: 6 hours

Servings: 4

Ingredients:

- 5 tablespoons butter

- 4 boneless chicken breasts

- Salt and pepper to taste

- 1 tablespoon parsley

- 1 teaspoon rosemary

Directions:

1. Melt the butter in the skillet. Season chicken with salt and pepper to taste. Brown all sides of the chicken for 3 minutes.

2. Transfer into the crockpot and sprinkle with parsley and rosemary. Cook on low for 6 hours or on high for 5 hours.

Nutrition:

Calories: 459

Carbohydrates: 1.17g

Protein: 61.6g

Fat: 21.5g

22.　Curry-Glazed Chicken

Preparation time: 3 minutes Cooking time: 9 hours

Servings: 12

Ingredients:

- ¼ cup butter, melted ¼ cup yellow mustard

- Salt and pepper to taste

- 2 tablespoons curry powder

- 1 whole chicken, cut up into pieces

Directions:

1. Place all ingredients in the crockpot. Mix everything to combine. Close the lid and cook on low for 9 hours or on high for 7 hours.

Nutrition: Calories: 119 Carbohydrates:3.5 g Protein: 10.5g Fat: 8.5g

23.   Roasted Chicken

Preparation time: 5 minutes

Cooking time: 8 hours

Servings: 8

Ingredients:

- 2 tablespoons olive oil

- 8 chicken breasts, skin and bones removed

- 1 cup parsley leaves, chopped

- 5 cloves of garlic, sliced

- Salt and pepper to taste

Directions:

1. Place foil in the bottom of the crockpot. Pour the olive oil. Season the chicken breasts with parsley leaves, garlic, salt and pepper.

2. Place in the crockpot and give a good mix. Close the lid and cook on low for 8 hours and on high for 6 hours.

Nutrition:

Calories: 526

Carbohydrates: 1.6g

Protein: 60.9g

Fat: 30.3g

24. Sun-Dried Tomato Chicken

Preparation time: 10 minutes

Cooking time: 8 hours

Servings: 10

Ingredients:

- 1 tablespoon butter

- 3 cloves of garlic, minced

- 4 pounds whole chicken, cut into pieces

- 1 cup sun-dried tomatoes in vinaigrette

- Salt and pepper to taste

Directions:

1. In a skillet, melt the butter and sauté the garlic until lightly browned. Add the chicken pieces and cook for 3 minutes until slightly browned.

2. Transfer to the crockpot and stir in the sun-dried tomatoes including the vinaigrette. Season with salt and pepper to taste. Close the lid and cook on low for 8 hours or on high for 6 hours.

Nutrition:

Calories: 397

Carbohydrates:9.4 g

Protein: 30.26g

Fat:14.1 g

25. Lime and Pepper Chicken

Preparation time: 4 hours

Cooking time: 8 hours

Servings: 4

Ingredients:

- ½ cup lime juice

- Salt and pepper to taste

- 3 tablespoons sucralose or stevia sweetener

- 4 chicken breasts, bones removed

- 1 tablespoon olive oil

Directions:

1. In a mixing bowl, combine the lime juice, salt, pepper, and sucralose. Marinate the chicken breasts for a few hours in the fridge.

2. Add the oil and give a good mix. Close the lid and cook on low for 8 hours or on high for 6 hours.

Nutrition:

Calories: 573

Carbohydrates: 4.7g

Protein:60.3 g

Fat:30.9 g

CHAPTER 6:

Meat

26. Cucumber and Pork Cubes Bowl

Preparation time: 15 minutes

Cooking Time: 4 Hours

Servings: 4

Ingredients:

- 3 cucumbers, chopped

- 1 jalapeno pepper, diced

- 1 red onion, diced

- 3 tablespoons soy sauce

- 1 tablespoon olive oil

- 8 oz pork tenderloin

- 1 cup of water

Directions:

1. Pour water in the Crock Pot. Add pork tenderloin and cook it on High for 4 hours. Meanwhile, mix the red onion with jalapeno pepper and cucumbers in the salad bowl.

2. In the shallow bowl mix soy sauce and olive oil. When the pork is cooked, chop it roughly and add in the cucumber salad. Sprinkle the salad with oil-soy sauce mixture and shake well.

Nutrition: Calories 163 Protein 17.4g

Carbohydrates 11.9g Fat 5.8g

27. Rosemary Beef

Preparation time: 15 minutes Cooking Time: 7 Hours

Servings: 2 Ingredients:

- 1 pound beef roast, sliced

- 1 tablespoon rosemary, chopped

- Juice of ½ lemon 1 tablespoon olive oil

- ½ cup tomato sauce

- A pinch of salt and black pepper

Directions:

1. In your Crock Pot, mix the roast with the rosemary, lemon juice and the other ingredients, toss, put the lid on and cook on Low for 7 hours. Divide everything between plates and serve.

Nutrition: Calories 210 Fat 5g Carbs 8g Protein 12g

28. Beef and Barley Sauté

Preparation time: 15 minutes

Cooking Time: 8 Hours

Servings: 6

Ingredients:

- ½ cup barley

- 1-pound beef brisket, chopped

- 2 tomatoes, chopped

- 1 onion, sliced

- 1 bell pepper, chopped

- 4 cups of water

- 1 teaspoon ground turmeric

- Directions:

1. Pour water in the Crock Pot. Add barley, beef brisket, tomatoes, onion, and bell pepper. Then add ground turmeric and close the lid. Cook the sauté on Low for 8 hours.

Nutrition:

Calories 217

Protein 25.6g

Carbohydrates 16.3g

Fat 5.3g

29.   Lamb and Fennel Mix

Preparation time: 15 minutes

Cooking Time: 4 Hours

Servings: 2

Ingredients:

- 1 pound lamb stew meat, roughly cubed

- 1 fennel bulb, sliced

- 1 tablespoon lemon juice

- 1 teaspoon avocado oil

- ½ teaspoon coriander, ground

- 1 cup tomato passata

- A pinch of salt and black pepper

- 1 tablespoon cilantro, chopped

Directions:

1. In your Crock Pot, combine the lamb with the fennel, lemon juice and the other ingredients, toss, put the lid on and cook on High for 4 hours. Divide the mix between plates and serve.

Nutrition:

Calories 263

Fat 12g

Carbs 7g

Protein 10g

30.   Mayo Pork Salad

Preparation time: 15 minutes Cooking Time: 4 Hours

Servings: 4

Ingredients:

- 7 oz pork loin

- 1 teaspoon salt

- 1 cup of water

- 1 cup arugula, chopped

- 2 eggs, hard-boiled, peeled, chopped

- 3 tablespoons mayonnaise

Directions:

1. Pour water in the Crock Pot. Add pork loin and close the lid. Cook the meat on high for 4 hours. After this, drain water and cut the pork loin into strips.

2. Put the pork strips in the big salad bowl. Add arugula and chopped eggs. Add mayonnaise and carefully mix the salad.

Nutrition:

Calories 196

Protein 16.6g

Carbohydrates 3g

Fat 12.8g

31. Ground Pork and Veggies

Preparation time: 15 minutes

Cooking Time: 8 Hours

Servings: 5

Ingredients:

- 2 cups ground pork

- 1 tablespoon minced garlic

- 1 green bell pepper, chopped

- 1 red bell pepper, chopped

- 1 zucchini, chopped

- 1 eggplant, chopped

- ½ cup cherry tomatoes, halved

- ½ cup keto tomato sauce

- 2 spring onions, chopped

- 1 teaspoon cayenne pepper

- ½ teaspoon salt

- ½ teaspoon ground coriander

- 1 tablespoon butter, softened

Directions:

1. In the crockpot, mix the pork with garlic, pepper and the other ingredients, toss, close the lid and cook for 8 hours on Low. Divide into bowls and serve.

Nutrition:

Calories 349

Fat 16.3g

Carbs 5.5g

Protein 13.8g

32. Herbed Lamb Loin Chops

Preparation time: 15 minutes

Cooking Time: 8 Hours

Servings: 1

Ingredients:

- 2 tablespoons of Butter melted

- 1 tablespoon of swerve

- ¼ cup of dill, diced

- 3 green onions, diced

- 1 tablespoon of Lemon peel, grated

- Salt and black pepper- to taste

- 1 lamb loin chop

Directions:

1. Start by putting all the fixings into your Crockpot.
   Cover its lid and cook for 8 hours on Low setting.
   Once done, remove its lid and mix well. Garnish as
   desired. Serve warm.

Nutrition:

Calories 298

Fat 14.4 g

Carbs 7.4 g

Protein 31.4 g

CHAPTER 7:

Vegetables

33. Spinach Lasagna

Preparation: 30 minutes

Cooking: 6 hours

Servings: 8

Ingredients:

- 14 ½ oz Canned diced tomatoes, undrained

- 25 ½ oz Organic tomato basil paste sauce

- 1 Coarsely chopped yellow bell pepper

- ¼ tsp Red pepper, crushed

- 9 Uncooked lasagna noodles

- 1 Thinly sliced zucchini

- 6 oz Shredded skimmed mozzarella cheese

- 1 ¼ cup Light ricotta cheese

- 4 oz Coarsely chopped fresh baby spinach

Directions:

1. Spray some cooking spray in the bottom of a 6-quart crock pot. In a medium bowl mix tomatoes, pasta sauce, bell pepper, crushed red pepper, and zucchini.

2. Spread a cup of tomato mixture on the bottom part of the crock pot. Layer the three lasagna noodles over the tomato mixture. Break the noodles so that you can easily layer the noodles.

3. Layer half portion of the ricotta cheese on top of the noodles. Sprinkle half the quantity of spinach and 1/4 cup of mozzarella cheese above the layer.

4. Top it with one-third portion of tomato sauce mixture. Repeat the layering process of noodles, cheese, and spinach for at least three layers.

5. Cover the crock pot and slow cook for 6 hours until the noodles become tender. Before serving, sprinkle mozzarella all over the lasagna and let it the cheese start melting.

Nutrition:

Calories: 440

Carbohydrate: 37g

Protein: 25g

Fat: 22g

34. Mediterranean Egg Plant Dish

Preparation: 15 minutes

Cooking: 9 hours

Servings: 8

Ingredients:

- 1 Diced onion

- 3 medium Peeled and cubed eggplants

- 1 can Diced tomatoes

- 2 Diced carrots

- 3 tbsp Veg oil

- 1 tbsp Tomato paste

- ¼ tsp Salt

- ½ tsp Pepper

- Paprika – as required

- Water – as needed

- ¼ cup Cilantro chopped

Directions:

1. In a large bowl put cubed eggplants, add water and salt. Stir it so that it can remove the bitter taste of eggplants. Pour oil into a saucepan and bring to medium heat.

2. Put the chopped onion and sauté until it turns light brown and keeps it aside. Now put canned tomatoes, tomato paste, and paprika into a 6-quart crock pot.

3. Remove the eggplants from the water and wash it under running tap water. Now put the eggplants along with the chopped carrots into the crock pot.

4. Transfer the sautéed onion into the crock pot and combine all the ingredients. Add a sufficient quantity

of water to cook the vegetables, or until the eggplants and carrots get entirely immersed.

5. Add pepper and salt as per your taste required. Set crock pot for 9 hours. Garnish with chopped cilantro before serving. Serve hot with rice and salad.

Nutrition:

Calories: 63

Carbohydrate: 4.1g

Protein: 0.6g

Fat: 5.2g

35. Ratatouille

Preparation: 25 minutes

Cooking: 6 hours

Servings: 6

Ingredients:

- 1 medium Eggplant, cut into ¾" size

- 2 tbsp Tomato paste

- 3 tbsp Olive oil

- 1 pound Plum tomatoes, medium dice

- ¼ tsp Freshly ground black pepper

- 1 large Yellow bell pepper cut into ¼ inch slices

- 8 oz Yellow summer squash, cut into 3/4 inch pieces

- 4 large cloves Garlic, finely sliced

- 1 Bay leaf

- 1 large Onion sliced into half

- 1 tbsp Fresh thyme leaves, chopped

- 1 ½ tsp Salt

- Fresh basil leaves, cut in ribbon size - for garnish

Directions:

1. In a large bowl put eggplant, one teaspoon salt and add water. Stir it and keep aside. Drain after 30 minutes. Rinse it under running tap water and place the eggplant over a paper towel.

2. Take a new bowl and whisk tomato paste, oil and the remaining salt along with black pepper.

3. Combine the drained eggplant, zucchini or squash, tomatoes, onion, bell pepper, thyme, garlic in a crock

pot. Add the tomato-oil paste mixture into the crock pot and combine. Add bay leaf.

4. Cover and slow cook for 4 hours until the vegetable becomes tender. After four hours, open up the lid and cook for one more hour to let the extra liquid evaporate.

5. Discard the bay leaf before serving. Garnish with fresh basil leaves before serving.

Nutrition:

Calories: 130

Carbohydrate: 15g

Protein: 3g

Fat: 8g

36.   Beans Chili

Preparation: 15 minutes

Cooking: 7 hours

Servings: 6

Ingredients:

- 1 large Yellow onion, chopped

- 2 tbsp Olive oil, extra virgin

- 1 medium Red sweet pepper, cored and chopped

- 2 large cloves Garlic, minced

- 1 medium Celery stalk, finely chopped

- 1 medium Yellow sweet pepper, cored and chopped

- 1 ½ tbsp Chili powder

- 1 tsp Cumin

- 28 oz Baked beans with liquid

- 1 large Carrot peeled and sliced into a ¼ inch

- 28 oz Tomatoes, drained and diced

- 15 oz Corn Kernels fresh or frozen

- 15 oz Black beans rinsed and drained

- ¼ tsp Kosher salt

- ¾ cup Unsweetened coconut milk

For Garnishing:

- ½ tsp Lime zest

- ¼ cup Fresh parsley leaves, chopped

- ½ cup Greek yogurt

- ½ cup Cheddar cheese

Directions:

1. Take a large skillet and heat olive oil on medium heat. Add garlic and onion to the skillet and sauté it until it becomes soft.

2. Add celery, red and yellow sweet pepper, chili powder, cumin and stir for about 3 minutes. Now transfer all these ingredients into a 6-quart crock pot crock pot.

3. Stir to combine all these ingredients. Cover the lid and slow cook for 7 hours. Before serving, garnish using lime zest, fresh Italian parsley leaves, cheddar cheese, and Greek yogurt.

Nutrition:

Calories: 720

Carbohydrate: 94g

Protein: 47g Fat: 22g

CHAPTER 8:

Soups & Stews

37. Catalan Stew

Preparation time: 15 minutes

Cooking time: 8 hours

Servings: 6

Ingredients:

- 2 chopped slices Pancetta

- 2 tbsp. Olive Oil (extra virgin)

- 3 pounds Chuck Roast

- 1 cup Red Wine (dry)

- 2 chopped Onions

- 3 cups Beef Broth (low sodium)

- 2 tbsp. Tomato Paste

- 4 minced cloves Garlic

- 2 crushed Cinnamon Sticks

- 4 sprigs Thyme

- 3 slices of peeled Orange

- 1 ounce chopped Dark Chocolate

- 3 tbsp. chopped Parsley

Directions:

1. Sauté pancetta in oil till crisp. Transfer it to the crock pot. Using the same pan, sauté beef.

2. Transfer beef to the crock pot as well. Now, sauté onion for 3 minutes. Add wine, tomato paste and vinegar to the sauté pan and stir to mix.

3. Transfer this wine mixture to the crock pot and sprinkle on the rest of the ingredients except parsley. Cook on "low" for 8 hours. Stir when done.

4. Add the chocolate and cook on "high" for 10 minutes. Remove cinnamon, orange peel and thyme. Serve after garnishing with parsley.

Nutrition:

Calories 421

Fat 26 g

Carbohydrates 16 mg

Protein 55 g

38.   Pork Stew Caribbean Style

Preparation time: 15 minutes

Cooking time: 7 hours

Servings: 4

Ingredients:

- 1 ½ pounds cubed Pork Loin

- 1 tbsp. Thyme (dried)

- ¼ tsp. Allspice (ground)

- White Pepper (ground)

- 1 pound Yukon Potatoes, quartered

- 3 diced Carrots

- 1-inch piece of Ginger Root, chopped

- 2 tsp. Worcestershire Sauce

- 1 chopped clove Garlic

- ½ cup sliced Scallions

- 1 cup diced Tomatoes

Directions:

1. Coat the pork with pepper, allspice and thyme. Place remaining ingredients except scallions in the crock pot.

2. Put in the pork along with the Worcestershire sauce. Place the tomatoes on top. Cook on "low" for 7 hours. Serve the stew with scallions.

Nutrition:

Calories 452

Fat 27 g

Carbohydrates 25 mg

Protein 50 g

39.   Fish Stew

Preparation time: 15 minutes

Cooking time: 4 hours

Servings: 6

Ingredients:

- 1 sliced Leek

- 2 tsp. Olive Oil (extra virgin)

- 1 sliced Onion

- 4 minced cloves of Garlic

- ½ cup of White Wine (dry)

- 4 Bay Leaves

- ¼ cup Water

- ½ tsp. Black Pepper (cracked)

- 1 piece Orange Peel

- 2 tbsp. chopped Parsley

- 1 ½ pounds of Haddock Fillets

- 12 ounces peeled Shrimp

Directions:

1. Arrange garlic, leek and onion on the bottom of crock pot. Add water and wine. Put in the peppercorn, orange peel and bay leaves.

2. Cook on "high" for 2 hours. Now, add shrimp and fish. Cook again on "high" for 2 hours. Remove the orange peel and bay leaves. Garnish with parsley and olive oil. Serve hot in heated bowls.

Nutrition:Calories 421Fat 26 g

Carbohydrates 16 mg Protein 55 g

40. Tuna and Red Pepper Stew

Preparation time: 15 minutes

Cooking time: 4 hours

Servings: 6

Ingredients:

- 1 tbsp. Olive Oil

- 1 chopped Onion

- 1 minced clove Garlic

- ½ cup White Wine (dry)

- ¼ tsp. Pepper Flakes (red)

- 14 ounce diced Tomatoes

- 1 tsp. Paprika

- 1 pound scrubbed red potatoes

- 2 sliced roasted Bell Peppers (red)

- 2 pounds of Tuna Fillet

- 3 tbsp. Cilantro (chopped)

Directions:

1. Except for paprika, tuna and peppers, place all the ingredients in the crock pot and cook on "high" for 2 hours.

2. Add paprika, tuna, and peppers. Cook again on "high" for 2 hours. Garnish with cilantro. Serve hot.

Nutrition:

Calories 107

Fat 3 g

Carbohydrates 15 mg

Protein 5 g

41.   Chipotle Squash Soup

Preparation time: 15 minutes

Cooking time: 4 hours

Servings: 6

Ingredients:

- 6 cups Butternut Squash (cubed)

- ½ cup chopped Onion

- 2 tsp. Adobo Chipotle

- 2 cups Chicken Broth

- 1 tbsp. Brown Sugar

- ¼ cup Tart Apple (chopped)

- 1 cup Yogurt (Greek style)

- 2 tbsp. Chives (chopped)

Directions:

1. Except yogurt, chives and apple, place all the ingredients in the crock pot. Cook on "low" for 4 hours. Now, in a blender or food processer, puree the cooked ingredients.

2. Transfer puree to crock pot. Add the yogurt and cook on "Low" for 20 more minutes. Garnish with chives and apples. Serve hot in heated bowls.

Nutrition:

Calories 102

Fat 11 g

Carbohydrates 22 mg

Protein 4 g

CHAPTER 9:

Snacks

42. Mussels Salad

Preparation time: 10 minutes Cooking time: 2 hours and 30 minutes Servings:

Ingredients:

- 1 pound mussels

- ½ cup veggie stock

- 2 teaspoons cayenne pepper

- 3 tablespoons lemon juice

- ½ cup olive oil

- 1 garlic clove, minced

- 2 handfuls mixed salad greens

- 1 avocado, pitted, peeled and cubed

- 1 red bell pepper, cut into thin strips

Directions:

1. In your crock pot, combine the mussels with the stock, cayenne and lemon juice, cover, cook on Low for 2 hours and 30 minutes, drain the mussels, transfer them to a salad bowl, add the oil, the garlic, salad greens, avocado and bell pepper, toss, divide into small cups and serve.

Nutrition: Calories 245 at 4g Carbs 16g Protein 8g

43. Olives Salad

Preparation time: 10 minutes

Cooking time: 2 hours

Servings: 6

Ingredients:

- 1 cup black olives, pitted

- 1 cup kalamata olives, pitted

- 1 cup green olives, pitted

- 3 cups salad greens

- 5 garlic cloves, minced

- A pinch of black pepper

- 2 tablespoons olive oil

- ½ cup veggie stock

- 1 teaspoon Italian seasoning

- 1 teaspoon lemon zest, grated

Directions:

1. In your crock pot, combine the black olives with the green ones and the kalamata ones. Add the garlic, black pepper, seasoning, lemon zest and stock, cover and cook on Low for 2 hours.

2. Transfer to a salad bowl, add the oil and the salad greens, toss, divide into small cups and serve.

Nutrition:

Calories 200

Fat 2g

Carbs 14g

Protein 6g

44.   Cauliflower and Jalapeno Dip

Preparation time: 10 minutes

Cooking time: 2 hours and 15 minutes

Servings: 6

Ingredients:

- 4 bacon slices, chopped and cooked

- 2 jalapenos, chopped

- ½ cup coconut cream

- 2 cups cauliflower rice

- ¼ cup cashew cheese, grated

- A pinch of salt and black pepper

- 2 tablespoons chives, chopped

Directions:

1. In your crock pot, mix bacon with jalapenos, coconut cream, cauliflower, salt and pepper, stir, cover and cook on Low for 2 hours.

2. Add cashew cheese and chives, cover and cook on Low for 15 minutes more. Divide into bowls and serve.

Nutrition:

Calories 182

Fat 3g

Carbs 7g

Protein 6g

45. BBQ Kielbasa

Preparation time: 10 minutes Cooking time: 4 hours Servings: 6 Ingredients:

- 2 cup tomato sauce

- ½ cup stevia 2 teaspoons mustard

- 1 teaspoon hot sauce

- 1 yellow onion, chopped

- 2 pounds kielbasa, sliced

Directions:

1. In your crock pot, mix kielbasa slices with tomato sauce, stevia, mustard, hot sauce and onion, stirs, cover and cook on Low for 4 hours. Divide kielbasa slices into bowls and serve as a snack.

Nutrition: Calories 200 Fat 3g Carbs 7g Protein 3g

46. Zucchini Bites

Preparation time: 10 minutes Cooking time: 2 hours Servings: 4

Ingredients:

- ½ cup tomato sauce 1 zucchini, sliced

- Black pepper to the taste

- A pinch of cumin, ground

- 1 tablespoon parsley, chopped

Directions:

1. In your crock pot, combine the zucchini with the tomato sauce, black pepper, cumin and parsley, cover, cook on Low for 2 hours, divide into small bowls and serve.

Nutrition: Calories 170 Fat 5g Carbs 8g Protein 7g

CHAPTER 10:

Desserts

47.   Mud Pie

Preparation time: 15 minutes

Cooking time: 2 hours

Servings: 6-8

Ingredients:

- Cooking spray

- 1 1/3 cups brown sugar, divided

- ½ cup butter, softened

- ½ cup plus 1/3 cup cocoa powder

- ¼ teaspoon salt

- 1/3 cup milk

- 1 cup flour 1 ½ cups water

Directions:

1. Grease generously the inside of crock pot with cooking spray. Divide sugar, putting each halve (about 2/3 cup each) in separate bowls.

2. In one bowl, mix butter, ½ cup cocoa powder, salt, and milk together. Add flour gradually and mix to make a smooth batter. Distribute mixture evenly in crock pot.

3. In second bowl, add remaining (1/3 cup) cocoa to sugar and mix. Add water and stir until sugar is dissolved. Pour this over batter in crock pot.

4. Cover and cook on high for 2 hours. Serve warm with toppings of your choice like ice cream, chocolate syrup, nuts or whipped cream.

Nutrition:Calories 602 Fat 26.6 g Carbs 84.4 g Protein 8.6 g

48. Blueberry Crisp

Preparation time: 15 minutes

Cooking time: 2 hours

Servings: 8

Ingredients:

- 1 cup almond flour

- ¼ cup coconut flour

- ¾ cup coconut sugar

- 1 teaspoon baking soda

- 1 teaspoon cinnamon

- 1/8 teaspoon sea salt

- 1 large egg, lightly beaten

- ¼ cup coconut milk

- 2 tablespoons coconut oil plus a little extra for greasing

- ½ cup pecans (or any nut of your choice, for example, chopped almonds, walnuts or cashew)

- 4 cups blueberries

- 1 tablespoon lemon juice

- 2 tablespoons maple syrup (optional, depending on the sweetness of blueberries)

- Zest of 1 lemon

Directions:

1. Mix the almond flour, coconut flour, coconut sugar, baking soda, cinnamon and sea salt in a bowl. In a separate bowl, whisk together the egg, coconut milk, and oil.

2. Stir the egg mixture into the flour mixture. Do not overmix. Line the inside of the crock pot with parchment paper and grease with oil.

3. Spread the dough evenly over the bottom. Sprinkle with nuts. Mix together the blueberries, maple syrup (if desired), zest and lemon juice. Pour over the dough.

4. Cook for 2 hours on high. Allow to set for at least 15 minutes before serving.

Nutrition:

Calories 313

Fat 17 g

Carbs 38.3 g

Protein 5.5 g

49. Cinnamon Pears

Preparation time: 15 minutes

Cooking time: 2 hours

Servings: 4

Ingredients:

- 5 pears, sliced into two 2 teaspoons of cinnamon

- 1 teaspoon nutmeg 2 tablespoons honey

- 4 tablespoons brown sugar

Directions:

1. In a crock pot, combine the pears, cinnamon, nutmeg, honey, and brown sugar. Cook for 2 hours on high. Sprinkle with more cinnamon before serving.

Nutrition:

Calories 658 Fat 13.3 g Carbs 144.5 g Protein 2.4 g

50.   Creamy Chocolate Treat

Preparation time: 15 minutes

Cooking time: 1 hour

Servings: 2

Ingredients:

- 2 ounces dark chocolate, cut in small chunks

- ¼ cup low-fat cream

- ½ teaspoon sugar

Directions:

1. In your crock pot, combine all the ingredients. Cook on high for 1 hour. Spoon the mixture into a serving bowl, and chill in the refrigerator. Serve cold.

Nutrition:Calories 115 Fat 10 g arbs 5.6 g Protein 2.4 g

Conclusion

You have to the end of this amazing cookbook, but always remember that this is not the end of your cooking journey with the crockpot; but instead, this is your stepping stone towards more cooking glory. We hope you have found your favorite recipes that are time-saving and money-saving.

The crockpot can be used in making homemade and custom-made buffets, even in catering services. You can use it for cooking for your staff for special occasions and for showing them how to cook a tasty and healthier dish for your guests well within their own crockpot.

Moreover, whether you are a newbie or an experienced cook, you are going to love this cookbook as it is packed with every conceivable taste. You have discovered more than 1000 recipes in this cookbook that you can put into practice using your crockpot. You can always customize the recipes to suit your taste buds, as you can make any recipe mild or hot, sweet or sour; you have all the freedom to make the recipes your own. The best thing about cooking using a crockpot is that you just need to add the main ingredients, and no other complicated cooking preparation is needed; the crockpot will add most of the other ingredients for you.

This crockpot cookbook covered all the recipes that are sure to make your heart happy and your taste buds happy as well. These meals are not just easy to make, but they will also save you hours of preparation and cleanup. The crockpot is also famous for its great nutritional value. It is the best nutritional value you will ever get. The high levels of healthy fats, proteins, and fiber you get when you cook using the crockpot are entirely natural, which everybody needs. Some of the ingredients are healthy enough to be consumed on their own.

When you are done with the crockpot recipes, just store them and access them whenever you need to. You could use them for a party, and your guests will love the recipes. They will love your attention to detail and your hospitality. You can invite them over, and when they are all set to leave, you will say that you must give them something of yours that you hope they will like, and now you know what recipes to include in such a thought that they will love and appreciate.

The only limit of the crockpot is your imagination and creativity. That is definitely why you fell in love with the crockpot. That is why you are going to expand your love for the crockpot through all these recipes.

After cooking with these recipes, you are sure that there are so many advantages of cooking with the crockpot. With all that said, use these recipes, and you will see that cooking is much easier than you have ever imagined it and that cooking can be fun as well. Go ahead and put your own signature twist on these recipes and let these recipes add magic to your life.

CPSIA information can be obtained
at www.ICGtesting.com
Printed in the USA
BVHW010912250421
605737BV00018B/215